FOOTNOTES

Footnotes

C. Perricone

BOATWHISTLE BOOKS

First published in 2018
by Boatwhistle Books
22 Gloucester Road
Twickenham
London TW2 6NE
United Kingdom

www.boatwhistle.com

Typeset in Bodoni by Boatwhistle

A catalogue record for this book
is available from the British Library

ISBN 978-1-911052-02-9

Printed in the United Kingdom by TJ International, Padstow,
on 80 gsm Munken Premium paper

MIX
Paper from
responsible sources
FSC
www.fsc.org   FSC® C013056

10 9 8 7 6 5 4 3 2 1

For Emily

I have sometimes thought of getting rid of these notes; but now they can never be unstuck. They have had almost greater popularity than the poem itself—anyone who bought my book of poems, and found that the notes to <u>The Waste Land</u> were not in it, would demand his money back.

T. S. Eliot, "The Frontiers of Criticism"

1.

The first footnote
Of <u>The Decline and Fall</u>
Refers to Dion Cassius.
Gibbon finds that Cassius,
At 1. liv. page 736,
Claims that Augustus,
Instead of leaving himself
And his army open
To Parthian fire,
Obtained an honorable treaty,
Along with the return
Of the standards and the prisoners
Once taken from Crassus,
As well as a few
Other non-specified deals.
According to the marble on which
Augustus told his story,
He "compelled" the Parthians
To accept his terms.
Unlike the Parthians
Who thought that fighting
Meant killing and dying,
Augustus realized that
The sword reifies the word.
As Gibbon suggests,
The meaning of "compelled"
Is typically equivocal,
Contingent upon and shaded by

The vanity of the one
Who utters it.
That time then
Was a prelude to
". . . the second century
Of the Christian era,
(When) the Empire of Rome
Comprehended the fairest . . . the earth,
And the most civilized . . . mankind."

2.

Seneca's Letter 114 to Lucilius
Is all about style,
About the questions of words
And about the questions of shirts,
The colors and the jewelry you choose,
A wife, a friend,
The slaves in your care,
How the sun passes through
The eye of your home.
Maecenas was no good,
Even though he was a friend
To Virgil and executive producer
Of the Age of Gold.
Just look at the way he walked,
How he desired to seem,
How he did not want his very own *vitia*,
I.e. his "blemishes," "imperfections,"
His "vices" to remain unexposed.
In the "Explanatory Notes"
Of the Select Letters,
Walter C. Summers comments
On 4, line 20 that
Seneca is the "chief authority
For the effeminacy of Maecenas' *character* . . ."
Summers furthermore mentions that
Seneca preserved (101.11)
"The ignoble poem in which M.
Prays for long life,

No matter how his body fares."
Look, even if my hand is "*debilem*,"
"Lame," "weak," "feeble," "frail,"
And my feet, too . . .
Tumors, "tumesc-ing" and so forth and so on,
"*Vita dum superest, bene est . . .*"
"As long as life remains, I'm glad . . .
And, that is, even if nailed to the cross."
Seneca says that Maecenas
Might have been a great man,
Had not his speech been
Wandering and licentious . . .
Had he sought to be felt not heard . . .
Had he not been both
So easily frightened and so easily pleased.

3.

You see although he might have
Gotten the idea from Dante,
It was Eliot who started it all,
More specifically the note on line 218,
Page 50 in the Harvest paperback,
The cheap shot at Tiresias
Out of <u>Metamorphoses</u>, Book III, 320ff:
The blind man who sees
What the sighted are blind to . . .
"The violet hour," as Eliot says,
The sailors, the draw of home, and so on.
In the "Notes on 'The Waste Land,'"
Eliot says: "The whole passage
(I.e. on Tiresias) from Ovid
Is of great anthropological interest."
Like a mantra: "so all women are one woman."
Because "the two sexes meet in Tiresias,"
He can see what the sighted are blind to . . .
But you see it's a joke.
Jupiter and Juno were joking around,
And sad to say, Tiresias got caught
In the connubial crossfire.
You knew from the start, he was a goner.
Jupiter claimed that women come higher than men,
With reckless, and as it were, concussive abandon.
Just look at their faces
And you'll see what I mean . . .
Juno at line 322 says that's not true.

The gods leave it up to the wise Tiresias to decide,
Since he has been both woman and man,
A tale of snakes, and so forth and so on . . .
Tiresias agrees with Jupiter.
Juno doesn't find the joking funny.
Thus, she strikes Tiresias blind.
Since not even the Almighty Father can
Unmake what other gods do,
In return for the lights lost to eternal night,
Jupiter endows Tiresias with the power
To see the future . . . .
Had Tiresias been truly wise,
He would have seen with his own eyes
That to joke with the gods is a no win,
And so is the sight of the seer . . .
So, all women are one.
So, the sexes meet in every man.
So, snakes shall bite their own tails.
So, Americans pretend to be English.
So, Romans pretend to be Greeks.
So, texts fade and dissolve into footnotes . . .
May we all one day find, if not jokes,
A peace that is possible to understand.
And so, may Eliot rest in peace:
"Shantih shantih shantih."

4.

After the index,
Which is described as
"Mainly prosopographical in character,"
Of the paperback edition
Of The Roman Revolution
By Sir Ronald Syme,
There are the family trees,
The literally horizontal
And vertical lines,
The names clinging,
A fragile foliage,
Paradoxically as it were
By the bonds of so
Many centuries of autumns,
Of the noble houses of Rome
And of the principal allies
Of the various men
Who then would lead.
Hence the stemma of the Metelli,
Compiled with the help
Of the tables of Munzer,
Tracing the sons of Crassus
And 3 of the 5 marriages
Of Pompeius Magnus . . .
And likewise depicted:
The kinsmen of Cato,
The family of Augustus . . .
Even a short, but helpful rendering

Of the blood lines
Of those who might have
Contributed to making Sejanus so cruel,
The very same Sejanus whom
Tiberius through Tacitus called
The "partner of my labor."
We all have many to thank
Not only for the content
But also for the structure
Of what we make of our lives,
And no one knew so
Better than Syme.
For the tone and treatment of his work,
He credits none other than
Sallust, Pollio, and Tacitus.
Naturally, the nature
Of Syme's subject matter dictates
That he mention
In the most glowing terms
Munzer for his work on
Republican family history,
Along with Groag, Stein,
Tarn's writings about
Antonius and Cleopatra,
And, of course, Anton von Premerstein's
Posthumous book,
<u>Vom Werden und Wesen des Prinzipats</u>.
Without the recognition
And broadcast of our debts,
We will never understand,
As Syme understood so well,

That only after you lose your *libertas*
Do you feel the pride of your destiny,
How the well-ordered state has
No need of great men,
That the spirit of a people
Is best revealed in the bass notes
Of its emotive terms,
And that oh, yes,
"The praise or blame of the dead
Rather than the living
Foreshadows the sad fate of literature"
In the cradle of imperial rule.

5.

Monday mornings
When the leaves outside
Are reds and yellows
And the dreams the night before
Were nightmares,
Only the pictures,
The glossies of the ruins
In the sun of long ago will do.
I want to follow only
The numbers of the photographs
In the picture books
Page by shining page
Of the resorts of
Pompeii and the city of Hercules . . .
Imagine the smart set
And the smart money
And the lovers who negotiated
The costs of desire
And then traded
Heart for heart . . .
Or sometimes sought
To steal two hearts for one
Without care for the bodies
That then might fall.
Number 3: The Porta Salinensis is the gate
To the road where the salt works were.
Number 5: The City Walls with traces
Still of the missile damage

Caused at the time of Sulla's siege.
Numbers 10 and 11:
The streets and their ruts . . .
The Forum, the Basilica, 15 and 21, respectively . . .
And the blue, blue sky above.
The bas reliefs at the Temple of Vespasian,
The bas reliefs at the baths.
The representations of the theatrical masks
As it were around every corner,
Their yawning mugs begging for
Pity and/or laughs,
The Villa of Mysteries
Built in the second century,
Its Dionysian Frieze,
The rituals of Dionysus,
The panels of terror,
The Satyrs, the women,
The guy with a prick and a half . . .
And down the road again,
The millstones worked by the slaves.
And always the blue, blue, sky . . .
Sulla said that
"Eros makes fools of the old
And slaves of the young."
That's according to Steven Saylor,
Roman Blood, page 243.
Maybe so . . .
However, for sure
There are Monday mornings
That come and go
And then come and go . . .

When only the pictures,
The ruins, the sun, etc. . . .
Only pictures in a picture book will do.

6.

Reynolds and Wilson write
That Suetonius wrote that
The study of grammar,
To the widest extent
Of that term,
Was first introduced
Into Rome by the scholar
Crates of Mallos,
Scholar of Homer's words,
Their ups and downs,
And the ups and downs
Of wandering and war.
He (i.e. Suetonius) claims that
Crates had come to Rome
On diplomatic business
Sometime around 168 B.C.,
Somehow slipped,
Was pitched into a sewer,
In which he broke his leg . . .
Reynolds and Wilson say
That Suetonius says
Crates never walked again,
His diplomatic career destroyed.
Thus, he turned his bad fortune
To good use . . .
By delivering lectures on poetry.
Reynolds and Wilson insist, of course,
That the influences of

Hellenistic culture on Rome
Were more complex and more entangled
Than the event of a broken bone.
From here on, however,
The big names begin
To take off and fly:
Lampadio, Stilo, Varro, Probus,
Flaccus, Quintillian, *et al.* . . .
The use of the critical signs
Derived from Aristarchus,
The interpretation of obsolete
Or difficult words . . .
What is authentic?
What ought the standard be?
Is "authorship," etymologized
From *auctor*, largely
Or merely a creative adoption of
Existing themes and plots
From other literature
To new and other intents and reasons why?
Of course, *auctor*, which
Comes from the verb *augere*,
Suggests not only "to increase,"
But also "the power to teach,"
"Weight," "support," "sale,"
"Responsibility," and "authority."
Reynolds and Wilson state
That scholars of all periods,
And often with the best intentions,
Have the power to "deprave"
As well as "emend" the texts

They handle and read.
However, the good news is
Neither the ill effects of fame
Nor the pens of pedants
Appear to have adulterated
Textual traditions nearly as much
As might have been feared.

7.

As late as the fourth century B.C.,
Travel was neither easy nor pleasant,
The pirates at sea, the inns,
The roads, the adventitious
Thing-in-itself of the weather's change,
The tongue, the skin . . .
That feel and taste of glue
Concomitant with each excursus
From the course of our routine.
Most who traveled did so
For a specific reason
And only when they had to.
They went from here to there
For this or that
And counted themselves lucky
If they ever made it home.
But according to Livy,
At the end of the summer of 167 B.C.,
Aemilius Paulus, commander-in-chief
Of the Roman army, victor against Macedon,
"Decided upon a tour of Greece,
[To behold] those things which,
Through their fame and reputation,
Had been magnified by hearsay
Into more than what the eye [can see] . . ."
Like his contemporaries, Paulus
Was not interested in panoramas,
Savage prospects, serrated files

Of snow-capped peaks, or
The beauty of boundless waste.
He wanted to see the past.
He wanted to see the famous harbor
In which had gathered
The thousand ships of Agamemnon's fleet,
The presence of the gods,
Phidias' statue of Zeus at Olympia,
The temples and sanctuaries,
The stadia and then the theaters
At Epidaurus, Athens, and Delphi . . .
And perhaps a side trip
To visit Apollo at Bassae
In the mountains above the coast,
Upon which shines the day's last light
Before that day's sun
Dreams again of another tomorrow
At the bottom of the sea.
Paulus had heard the unspeakable rumor that
The gods, too, were travelers,
Moving further and further north.
Like all the tourists who will ever be,
He wanted to believe that rumor untrue . . .
The gods and the cold so cold that
The wind could not penetrate the fog,
And beyond a continent whose rivers
Filled the Atlantic with silt,
And whose people looked upon
The known world, the world of Aemilius Paulus,
As an island, a mere circle more or less,
Around which one travels only round and round.

8.

The figures on the capacity
Of the Circus Maximus vary.
Pliny in his <u>Natural History</u>, XXXVI, 102
Claims two hundred fifty thousand
After the time of Nero,
Whereas Dionysius of Halicarnassus, III, 68
Estimates the spectators at one fifty
Under the principate of Augustus . . .
Born, that is, Caius Octavius
Posthumously, Augustus the Divine.
Still the debate remains open:
<u>A Topographical Dictionary of Ancient Rome</u>,
Oxford, 1929 by Platner and Ashby
Range the seating capacity from a hundred forty
To three hundred eighty thousand.
In any case, you can imagine
All those people, the sounds
And the smells of them,
A breath as it were with a life of its own,
The horses and chariots straining to run,
The play of the gods and the grandeur of the place,
The man and the beast he drives,
And then always the element of the unforeseen . . .
Outside, of course, the wine merchants,
The caterers and pastry cooks,
The women who fuck for money,
And the men who will plot
Your life by the stars . . .

I should mention that Suetonius in the <u>Lives</u>
Says at "Domitian" 4,3 that during
The *ludi saeculares*, i.e. the centennial games,
He, Domitian, ran a hundred races a day.
This was done not only obviously
In celebration of the 100 years in itself,
Each race a metaphor for each glorious year,
But also because of
The falsely conceived idea that
The more you have the opportunity to wager
The more predictable the future shall become.

9.

It's the play among texts
That grabs your attention,
The play played softly,
The conversation
At the bottoms of pages
In the numbers
Of the corners of paragraphs
Across the many spans of sunsets
Between professors
At Oxford and Leipzig
Who've professed among echoes . . .
And poets who've lived in dives.
Juvenal hated women.
It's everywhere in the Satires,
But especially in 6,
The senator's wife doing the gladiator
While the senator's out of town,
The well-bred bitch, the athlete,
The corrupt mother, then the cunt with a whip,
And perhaps a woman who is also a man . . .
J. P. V. D. Balsdon in his Roman Women:
Their History and Habits
Asserts quite correctly that
The writers of ancient Rome were men,
The historians, the poets, and satirists,
All were men . . .
"And it is a thousand pities"
That there's not been left behind

One woman's record
Of the sunsets of her days.
As Balsdon suggests,
What a treat it would be
To read the record Tacitus read
Of Agrippina the Younger's own words,
Which she wrote and published,
The sunsets of her own sad story,
A story neither copied nor conceived,
Just a report of a chance
In a swerve among swerves,
And yet a story just the same . . .
Her words, her son—the Emperor Nero, her family . . .
Lost words which never will have found the play
To which such words should have been allowed.

10.

B. L. Gildersleeve and Gonzalez Lodge,
The former Sometime Professor of Greek
In the Johns Hopkins University,
The latter Sometime Associate Professor of Latin
In Bryn Mawr College,
Are the authors of <u>Latin Grammar</u>,
Everything from chapters on letters and syllables
To the inflections of nouns, adjectives, and verbs
To the tenses and moods of relative clauses,
The varieties of conditionals, the historical infinitive,
The figures of prosody—the pump of a language's
    lines,
The forms of versification:
Saturnian verse, the Anapestic rhythms,
The Cretic, the Ionic, and all the moves of Bacchus
    himself . . .
By means of the <u>Latin Grammar</u> all your questions
Will bear a crisper tone.
You will understand the active and passive voices,
(Why, according to Ovid,
"The fire is betrayed by its own light.")
And at the same time come to be reconciled
That no linguistic distinctions are eternal,
That intransitive verbs of passive signification,
Although patently active must be construed
Passive nonetheless.
You will find peace therein:
"Seek thy dwelling at eventide."

You will find the commonsensical claim that
"Bread and water is what nature calls for,"
The ambiguities and impossibilities of love:
How lovers send lovers
To fetch pearls from the sea.
There are paradoxes to enjoy:
"The height of right is the height of wrong."
The mistakes to puzzle over:
"No bad man is happy."
And then just a simple fact:
"Hamilcar was killed nine years
After he came to Spain."
You will learn that elision
Is more frequent in the Iambic Senarious
Than in the Dactylic Hexameter,
That Diaeresis, like Caesura,
Serves to distribute the masses of verse
And thus, prevent monotony.
You will learn that you never need
Again be embarrassed that
As a child among other children
You couldn't find the words
To excuse yourself . . . and how you cried,
That all the forms of expression
Are luckily forever beyond the imagination's grasp,
And that the history of those forms
Is the legacy of our ancestors' virtues,
As well as their crimes.

11.

Ibid., page 338,
Which is
An abbreviation for
Ibidem, which means
"In the same place,"
Or more emphatically:
"In that very place,"
Or: "just there . . ."
I.e. in Gildersleeve and Lodge,
I.e. which is
An abbreviation for
Id est, which means
"This (or that) thing is,"
Which if you think about it
Has a Thomistic,
Or perhaps better,
A Heideggerian ring to it.
Of course, "*id est*"
Is close to
But not quite the same as
Viz., which is
An abbreviation for
Videlicet, which means variously
"It is plain to see,"
"Evidently," "namely,"
And sometimes ironically: "no doubt."
By the way,
The "z" in viz.,

You might be interested
To know
Is a corruption
Of the medieval
Latin contraction for
Et, which means
"And."
Anyway . . .
At page 338, entry 536
Gildersleeve and Lodge write
About how the participle
Is used after verbs
Of perception and representation,
An instance of such being
From Cicero's <u>De Finibus</u> III, 2, 7:
"*Catonem vidi in bibliotheca*
Sedentem multis circumfusum
Stoicorum libris,"
Which Gildersleeve and Lodge say means,
"I saw Cato sitting
In the library with
An ocean of Stoic books
About him."
But, which I would say means,
"I saw Cato sitting
In the library
Surrounded by the
Many books of the Stoics."
Or might it be:
The Stoics' books
"Poured around" him,

"Overwhelming," "flowing,"
"Closing" . . .
Such details, of course,
Are not insignificant,
A question of
Literal and figurative meaning,
When to choose one
And not the other,
And how easily you
Can be deceived into
Thinking you're choosing . . .
Swimming or drowning . . .
And the potential for
Drowning others, i.e.
Depending on how you read.

12.

Charles Merivale, D.D.,
That is, Doctor of Divinity,
One time Dean of Ely, writes that
"Catalina's adherents
Were mostly young men . . ."
Filii familiarum,
That is, sons of slaves.
Merivale also notes that
Cicero calls them
Libidinosa et delicata juventus
In <u>Ad Atticus</u> i. 19,
"*Libidinosa*" meaning merely
"Luxurious" or "lustful,"
"*Delicata*" subtly and variously
Insinuating "delightful," "charming,"
"Soft," "dainty," or "spoiled."
These were uncertain times
For the Roman Republic,
Especially for the *juventus*,
I.e. for the youth and their gangs . . .
And at night the streets were dark.
Merivale's edition of <u>Catalina</u>
By Caius Sallustius Crispus
Was originally printed in 1870.
Now in its 25th edition
Published by Macmillan,
It is still intended
"For use in schools."

13.

The Latin Sexual Vocabulary
By J. N. Adams and published by
The Johns Hopkins University Press
Contains chapters entitled
"Designations of the Female Genitalia,"
"*Culus* and its Synonyms," etc.,
Along with sections pertaining to
Sociolinguistic and contextual variation,
Defecation, Some elliptical euphemisms,
Metaphors, Metonymy, Basic obscenities,
And so forth and so on . . .
For example, "*Lingo*,"
Says Adams, "was not inherently obscene."
And, indeed, this is confirmed by
The Oxford Latin Dictionary,
Henceforth: OLD.
The direct objects of *lingo*,
Meaning "to tongue (it)" or "to lick," therefore,
Might be "salt" or "honey,"
As well as the well-established
Sexual applications,
Such as "cunt," "asshole," or "balls."
Adams points out,
One might say, gratuitously,
That in the latter sense,
Lingo "had no doubt acquired
An offensive tone."
If one consults CIL,

Meaning the <u>Corpus Inscriptionum Latinarum</u>,
Meaning the <u>Body of Latin Inscriptions</u>,
One would find that "*cunnum*," meaning "cunt,"
Comes before "*lingere*," meaning "to lick,"
Whereas "*mentulam*," meaning prick,
Comes after the verb.
Apparently both frequency of use and word order
Suggest that the phrase "*cunnum lingere*"
Is the older of the two.
And that is probably true.
However, I suggest that
There are perhaps meanings embedded here
That many of us would rather not discuss.

14.

Bearded soldiers are depicted
On Trajan's column,
And the long beard, in particular,
Was part of the inappetent,
Suggestive of transcendent, and wise
Appearance affected by
The professional philosopher
Under the empire . . .
Or so says Seneca
In the Letters, 5, 2.,
As well the first Satire
Of Persius, line 133.
It should be noted that Persius,
Who died at 27, has left us
A mere 700 lines of poetry,
Upon which his reputation rests . . .
A strand of a thread
In a breath of chance,
Which is the difference between
Immortality and oblivion.
In any event, a young man's first beard
Was cut by scissors only,
Offered to the gods
Under the strict codes of rite
As it were . . . a surrealistic fruit,
The deposit of one's beard,
A renunciation of boyhood
And a resignation to

The limits of one's own age.
The gods having been satisfied,
A razor was now permitted
With which to shave,
The razor in the first century A.D.,
As you might imagine,
A most crude and inefficient edge . . .
Hence the Roman man,
Especially the well-born,
Not inclined, with reason, to trust
His fellow citizen,
Was forced by the tacit dictates of fashion
And of religion, of course,
To place himself in the hands of specialists,
Barbers, i.e. *tonsores*, to whom routinely
He would expose his neck . . .
Gellius at IX, 2
Also points out that the beard was worn
By charlatans and beggars
Who posed as philosophers
And pretended like philosophers
To conceal themselves
From the slips of time.

15.

In the Cambridge University Press edition
Of the "Cupid and Psyche" section of
Apuleius' The Transformations of Lucius
Otherwise Known as The Golden Ass,
The editor, E. J. Kenney,
Emeritus Professor of Latin
In the University of Cambridge,
Notes in his "Commentary" of
Liber 5, section 11, line 4
That "*lupulae*" is an Apuleian diminutive
Of "*lupa*," which means she-wolf.
The point is that these perfidious whores,
Namely, the gorgeous Psyche's older sisters,
Are up to no good.
They are trying to persuade Psyche
To look straight into the face of Love.
Love, of course, replies succinctly:
non videbis si videris,
Which must be prolixly rendered into English:
"You will not see (my face), if once you will have
     seen it."
I construe "*videris*" to be future perfect.
Hence a nice illustration
Of what the grammarians call
The future conditional, more vivid.
As Kenney says: once you see Love,
"He will disappear;
The oracular paradox emphasizes the warning

Against Psyche's *curiositas*,
Her passion to know what
She is forbidden to know."
Kenney furthermore says,
There is another layer of meaning here,
Viz., Psyche will not recognize Love
If she sees him, that is,
The revelation of the true nature of love . . .
For which I, too, have found myself
To be so little prepared
Either to recognize or to know
And have thought, too,
Especially in hotel rooms
Far away from home,
May be forbidden by the gods.

16.

In the well-known battle
Between Caesar and Vercingetorix,
Noted military historian
And author of <u>Beyond the Rubicon:</u>
<u>A History of Early Rome</u>,
Major Reginald Hargreaves
Explains that the secret of Caesar's
Victory and his subsequent
Rule of Gaul
Lay in his genius to build . . .
The redoubts and barriers,
Which enabled him to cover himself
Against simultaneous attack
From the front and rear,
The wet and dry ditches
Bristling with *cervi* and *stimuli*,
The booby traps, so quaintly
Nicknamed by the soldiers,
Concealed among the branches
Of the trees having been felled,
Horns like stags' and spikes
To penetrate and tenderize the barbarian's
Abdomen, heart, and thigh . . .
Thus, perhaps to discourage
His urge for more and higher ground.
Hargreaves notes on page 266 with support from
<u>The Two Worlds Review</u>, May 1, 1858 that
"In the course of erecting their field works

The Legionaries shifted 2 million meters of earth."
I take it that the Major means
More precisely "2 million *cubic* meters" . . .
Hence notwithstanding
The Major's stiff upper lip,
A ball-breaking job if one considers
That we're talking here
Merely shovels and the power in
The muscles of the human back,
Especially the shoulders,
And the persistence of
And the skill in how well
Man by man a man shall place his feet.
On the cover of <u>Beyond the Rubicon</u>,
A Mentor Book, published in 1967,
The blurb reads: "A lively survey . . .
The development of an empire,
Based upon the historical and military
Accounts of the time."
It might also be mentioned that
Hargreaves is the editor
Of <u>Great English Short Stories</u>,
As well as author of
<u>Famous Duels and Assassinations</u>,
And <u>Women at Arms</u>.

17.

In the Proem of Book II
Of Lucretius' De Rerum Natura,
I.e. On the Nature of Things,
Leonard and Smith, editors,
Madison: The University of Wisconsin Press,
First printing, 1942, comment that
Lines 1 and 2 express a thought
"Proverbial in character,"
(See also Archippus, fragment 43)
In which he (Lucretius) says:
"How sweet to view the ocean from the land,
O mother, if one never sails thereon."
Naturally you should never travel by sea,
If you can avoid it,
Its surfaces, as the accusative plural
"*Aequora*" suggests, whipped up and disheveled
By the fortunes, favors, and rumors
Of the winds.
It's not just the seas, however,
That concern Archippus, Lucretius, and others . . .
As a matter of fact, as lines 7 and 8 say:
". . . *nihil dulcius est bene quam munita tenere
edita doctrina sapientum templa serena*."
The tough word, here, to translate is
The quite ordinary "*tenere*."
The reason is that although it literally
Means "to hold," it also means
"To be master of," "to occupy,"

"To hold in the mouth," "to hold in the hand,"
"To land on," "not to swerve from," "to understand."
Hence ". . . nothing is sweeter than
To occupy the fortified places,
The serene sanctuaries,
To understand the published teachings of the wise,
Perhaps hold them in your mouth,
To be the master of them, or to hold them in your
hand . . ."
It's a well-known line,
But that doesn't make it any easier
To get what it means.
It is also interesting that
In the same Book II at line 215
Where Lucretius begins his famous
Discussion: *De Clinatione Motus*,
That is, "Concerning the Swerve of Motion,"
He says that without the *clinamen*,
The swerve in the nature of things,
The atoms of this world
Would have fallen indefinitely
Through the void never having bumped
Into one another and never
Would have bumped again and again . . .
And thus, nature would have never created
Anything, neither temples nor seas.

18.

Around 110,
Robin Lane Fox points out:
Pliny, that is, the Younger,
Wrote to his Emperor, Trajan,
Of the ever-widening
Presence of the spread
Of the Christian religion.
He thinks the situation
Worthy of the Emperor's attention,
Because of the number
Of potential dangers
And the danger in numbers,
The air rife with hazard,
Experiment, risk, and trial,
The land across Turkey
And the clouds of the Black Sea.
At 10,96,9 of the Letters,
Pliny says that "Many"
Of all orders, ranks, and rule,
Of all stages of life,
And even of each sex
Are called and will
Be called into the Christian trial . . .
There's a sense in Pliny's tone that
They're everywhere:
The superstition, its infection
Transmitted by touch,
Wanders throughout

The cities, he says . . .
The villages, and the fields.
Pliny, normally so cool, says
That he had never seen a superstition
So "excessively bad," "*pravam immodicam.*"
Trajan wisely points out in his response
That no general policy can be established
To stop the spread of Christianity . . .
Or anything else for that matter.
I should mention three things:

1. Superstition to the Roman meant
    Any religion not authorized by the state.
2. On page 727, Fox recommends
    "H. Chadwick's masterly <u>The Early Church</u>,"
    Published in 1968.
    Chadwick says that
    One of the reasons
    For the Church's success
    Was its money smarts . . .
3. Fox's book, entitled <u>Pagans and Christians</u>,
    Was published by Harper & Row, 1986.

19.

In 1898, the American Book Company
Of New York, Cincinnati, and Chicago
Put out a nicely crafted edition of
<u>Captivi, Trinummus, et Rudens</u>,
Replete with woodcuts of
Thalia, the muse of comedy,
Satyrs, masks, and coins,
Ruins of the Ionic Temple of Lycia,
And the head of Olympian Jove . . . ,
The plays by Plautus in Latin
With critical and explanatory
Notes in English
By C. S. Harrington, M.A.
Harrington, writing in 1870,
States that the three plays
Presented, here, are Plautus' best,
Well illustrative of his style
And "comparatively free from
The blemishes and immoralities
That are often found in writings
Of this class in every age."
In the same vein later in his preface,
Harrington says it is a good idea,
Good for the soul as it were,
"To break up sometimes
The sobriety of Philosophy and History
With the imagery and humor of the Stage."
As for his "Notes,"

Harrington says in his most paean-ic tone,
That his "have sometimes been suggested
By those he has consulted."
By this he means, of course,
The work especially of Fleckeisen,
As well as all the other Plautus scholars,
Their hours alone, working the variations,
The riffs of the academe,
The passion for allusions, orthography,
Case and tense, their endings,
And so forth and so on . . .
The utter bulk and strata,
The condensations and elaborations,
The strands and the weaves
And the indications and moods
Of the labor and time of others . . .
All for the sake of bringing to you
The inharmonious numbers and careless prosody
Of Titus Maccus Plautus, Roman playwright . . .
How from jest to jest he aimed
To make the Romans laugh.

20.

In Plautus, *op. cit.*, p. 227.,
Harrington, referring to line 290
In Actus II of the <u>Captivi</u>,
Comments on the use of *genio*
The ablative of *genius*.
He says: "Every Roman
Had his own genius . . ."
That peculiar one implicit in every life
To which each of us owes everything,
And especially on birthdays:
Libations of wine, incense,
And garlands of rich scent, tint, and hue.
One's *genius* should not, however, be confused
With the *Manes*, *Lares*, and *Penates*.
Manes, according to the <u>OLD</u>,
"The spirits of the dead,
Regarded as minor supernatural powers,"
Sometimes also meaning, "ashes," or "doom."
Lares, "protectors" variously of the state,
Roads, crossroads, hearth, and home.
Penates, the embodiment in images,
Legible to the illiterate,
The material circumstances
And destiny of the household.
The latter three have the common feature
Of protecting life once it occurs,
Whereas the former, i.e. one's genius,
Produces life, one's own understudy,

A secret, "second or spiritual self,"
The gift for being unhappy
And the power, mixed with one's own saliva,
To choreograph such unhappiness
Into a moment of one's own dance.
Although Harrington fails to do so,
It should be noted that *genius* is
Derived from *gigno*, meaning
"To bring into being (or)
Create (living creatures),"
That is, again, according to the <u>OLD</u>.
Also derived from *gigno* are
Genitalis, *genitor*, *genitura*,
Genetrix, *genitabilis*, etc.
All orbiting around:
Reproduction, procreation, father,
Genitals, semen, horoscope,
Neptune, and inborn . . .
By the way *op. cit.* is an abbreviation
For *opere citato*, i.e. "in the work cited."
Also, it is interesting to know
That in my edition of Plautus,
There was left behind a bookmark,
From "The Rosery [*sic*] Flower Shop, Albany, N.Y.,"
It would seem, circa late 18 hundreds,
The frontispiece inscribed:
"Ginnie Neal, Class of '97, March 30, '95."

21.

The Harvard University Press
Did well to publish
<u>The Healing Hand:</u>
<u>Man and Wound in the Ancient World</u>
By Guido Majno, M.D., concerning
Both how tough and frail the body,
Its network of nerve and teeth,
How it shall clean itself
By means of its curd,
And then excel all the foreign bodies
That might invade it
By its very own power to burn.
In tenth-century handwriting,
A page in the manuscript of <u>De Medicina</u>
By Cornelius Celsus
Describes the signs of acute inflammation,
Which still hold true today:
"*Rubor et tumor cum calore et dolore*," meaning:
"Redness and swelling with heat and pain."
Celsus points out that chest pain,
Long before the discovery of antibiotics,
Might be so severe that
The accumulation of pus
In the pleural cavity
Would produce signs of visible inflammation . . .
Our lungs, our time,
And the sky above
Purified and consumed

Through the muscle and bone,
Cooked and then boiled up
To a head . . .
From the lungs to the bone
From the bone to the muscle
From the muscle to the skin.
In another line quoted by Majno,
Celsus defines "acute" for us.
He says acute inflammations or diseases
Are those that:
"*Cito vel tollunt hominem, vel ipsi cito finiuntur—*"
How elegant and also how so very concise.
The sentence is most often translated:
"(Acute diseases) either knock off a man quickly
Or they themselves are quickly knocked off."
Given the use of "*tollere*"
There is the sense that a man will be
Lifted up in some way
By the very thing that
May be eating him up alive . . .
Precisely in what sense, however,
Is not at all clear.

22.

Sometimes you have to quote in full
In order not to miss the full sense
Of what the author's got to say . . .
It's a question of piety,
A loyalty, a reverence to
The sources of one's being,
Which the Romans understood so well,
Who understood so well that
The ideal in a polyglot world
Is to understand all languages
And speak only one . . .
In Book I of The Gallic War
Caesar writes in *oratio obliqua*,
I.e. in indirect discourse:
"*Consuesse enim deos immortales,*
Quo gravius homines ex commutatione rerum doleant,
Quos pro scelere eorum ulcisci velint,
His secondiores interdum res
Et diuturniorem impunitatem concedere."
Caesar's point is clear, as usual,
And so, too, his noble sense of humor
Concerning the mortality of great deeds.
However, the translation of the passage
Somehow inevitably eludes
More than what reasonably seems acceptable,
Not only the subtle ties between men and gods
But also the redolent elegance of the alpha text.
In the Loeb Classical Library, Edwards offers

The following: "for it was the wont
Of the immortal gods to grant
A temporary prosperity and a longer impunity
To make men whom they purposed
To punish for their crime smart the more
Severely from a change of fortune."
I would offer the following:
"In fact, the immortal gods are accustomed
To grant greater good fortune sometimes
And longer lasting safety to those men
Whom they want to punish for a crime
In order that those men suffer more severely
From the change in the nature of things."
Caesar understood the gods well.
He understood by heart that hope
Lay not beyond the clouds
But is of and within
Those very clouds' muggy substance.
In principle, it is in the nature of the gods
To instill in us the fear of dying young
As the greatest fear,
And yet offer no consolation to the old . . .
The very same gods,
As it were Epicurean stand ups,
Who fashioned mankind
Superior to all other living species
In so far as only man is disgusted
By the smell of the filth of another . . .
And yet again delights excessively
In the smell of his own.

23.

The English word "index"
Comes from the Latin masculine word
"*Index*," derived from "*indicere*," meaning
"To give formal notice of," etc.,
And with family resemblances to
"*Iudex*," meaning "judge."
"*Index*," itself, is defined in the <u>OLD</u>
As "one who reveals or points out;
One who betrays a secret, an informer,
A look-out man . . . a marker, digest, or list,"
The pieces of a man, which both
Betray and inform in an index of proper names,
The names, the events, the descriptions,
The numbers of the pages, of the chapters,
The numbers of the paragraphs,
And the lines indicated in between . . .
No doubt among the best editions of <u>The Annales</u>
Is <u>Libri Annalium Cornelii Taciti,</u>
I.e. <u>The Books of the Annales of Cornelius Tacitus</u>,
Edited with introduction and notes by H. Furneaux,
Part of the Clarendon Press Series
Published in Oxford at the Clarendon Press, 1892.
In the index like shards
In alphabetical order among ruins . . .
The secrets on Scipio,
The entries on Livia, Germanicus,
The digest of the information about
The betrayals of Tiberius,

Both in the subjective and objective genitive
Senses of the meaning of "of ":
"Tiberius Claudius Nero, after-
Wards Tiberius Caesar, stepson
Of Augustus . . .
Loaded with honours, I, 4, 4;
Sent to the East . . .
Nine times in Germany . . .
Bountiful in gifts to some, I,
75, 4 . . .
Harsh . . .
Chiefly . . .
Blamed . . .
Declines . . .
His residence in Capreae,"
And so forth and so on . . .
The certainty that the text
Will fill in the blanks,
The doubt that any "list" is ever complete.
And, of course, the wonder that
What all the pagings
Through all the indexes
That might ever be
Is all about . . .
Is the "formal notice" that . . .
You yourself are the "look-out man" for whom
You have been looking all along.

24.

In Act 4, scene 14
Of <u>Antony and Cleopatra</u>,
Antony speaking to Eros,
Soon his mentor of death,
Speaks of the Queen's heart
He thought he had, did have,
And always will . . .
Perhaps speaking also of himself, thus:
"Sometimes we see a cloud that's dragonish,
A vapour sometimes, like a bear or lion,
A towered citadel, a pendant rock,
A forked mountain, or blue promontory
With trees upon't, that nod unto the world,
And mock our eyes with air.
Thou hast seen these signs;
They are black vesper's pageants."
This is the same Antony whom Cicero describes in
His *oratio*, meaning "speech,"
"The Oration against Marc Antony,"
Also known as "The 4th Phillipic,"
That Antony who runs away "*ardens odio vestri*", i.e.
"Burning with your (the people's) hatred",
"*Cruentus sanguine civium Romanorum*", i.e.
"Bloody with the blood of the citizens of Rome",
"*Cruentus*" meaning both "bloody" and "blood-thirsty,"
Both stained and wounded
And yet wanting the blood of more . . .
The Laurel Shakespeare series was published by Dell,

The <u>Selected Orations and Letters of Cicero</u>,
Scott, Foresman and Company, Chicago and New York,
Their pages now tattooed with mold,
Their spines crumbling into the sands,
Out of which they long ago rose . . .
Their unmistakable odor of both darkness and fire,
Their desiccated touch which clarifies
Both loathing and love.

25.

The words, that is, Suetonius',
Come at you in this way:
"*Accesserunt tantis ex principe*
Malis probisque quaedam et fortuita."
Of all the words and order in the world,
Suetonius chose the above for
The first line of 39 in Book 6
In the life of Nero.
Word for word they come at you
Close to gibberish:
"They came to so great from the Princeps
Evils and shameful acts
Certain and accidental things."
A sense of something being said somehow,
Like a simple tune concealed
In the ornamentation and heat
Of an all-night jam.
You've gotta shuffle and re-shuffle
To make sense out of words,
Both a three-card monte of the mind
And a shell game,
In which the eye is always
Quicker than the hand,
And still tends to err.
From Graves the hand appears:
"Fate made certain unexpected additions
To the disasters and scandals of Nero's reign . . ."
"Fate" in the sense that Nero's atrocities

Caused an injured Nature to respond . . .
But in Suetonius, Fate is nowhere to be found.
Only *quaedam et fortuita*,
Viz. the neuter nominative plural,
A universe in which exist "things,"
A plurality of "certain things
And casual, i.e. accidental things," nothing
Resembling a singular cosmic thingamajig,
Or even a Big Woman or Man.
So how about:
"Even certain accidental things came to
Or were added to the evils and to the shameful acts
That came out of the Princeps, i.e. Nero,"
Viz. a repetition of the dative sense of "to,"
Perhaps a more adequate, if not complete,
Substitution for the centerpiece
The dative case occupies in Suetonius's own hand . . .
Meantime, Suetonius says
Because of one autumn's pestilence
30,000 funerals appeared in the register of Libitina.
Of course, *pestilentia* is gorgeously vague,
Meaning either "bad air," or "plague."
According to Joseph B. Pike,
Professor of Latin in the University of Minnesota,
"In the temple of Venus Libitina, [the goddess of
    death],
Everything requisite for burials was kept. . . ."
It was the death store to which
Everyone who died in Rome must pay.

26.

Sir Mortimer Wheeler distinguishes well
In his <u>Roman Art and Architecture</u>
Between the Greek and Roman temple.
He says that
The Greek temple from the 7th cen. B.C. on
"Consisted of an oblong sanctum
With a porch at both ends
And a surrounding colonnade . . ."
Low stone platform,
Essentially symmetrical all around,
Its overall function ill-defined . . .
Rather than mere coruscation,
A mild morning's shower
In an otherwise always dry-ish June.
The Roman temple, however,
Sir Mortimer claims,
Derived from the same tradition,
Was nevertheless of a different mind.
The podium was lofty, 9 to 10 feet high,
As examples from Tunisia and Libya tell.
The colonnaded porch
Deep and dominating was
Suitable to large and dramatic
Swathes of shadows . . .
And like the movie set,
The Roman pattern was two dimensional,
Emphasizing length and width,
Thus, leaving depth in the eyes of the beholder . . .

The point: to make the temple a stage,
To make it flat in order
To draw and to command
The members of the assembly
Up front and below,
Jostling among themselves,
Forever fighting for position . . .
Who had paid for their tickets,
The palpable tokens of their right
To laugh, to pray, and then find
Comfort in the safety of their homes.

27.

Sometimes the preface
And the table of contents
Are enough:
"Part I:
An Outline of the History
Of the Latin Language."
"Part II:
Comparative-Historical Grammar."
The sections in Part I:
"Latin and the other
Indo-European Languages."
"The Proto-Latins in Italy."
"The Development of
The Literary Language."
"Plautus and Terence."
"Vulgar Latin."
And "The Latin of
The Followers of Jesus Christ
King of the Jews."
The sections in Part II:
"Phonology."
"Morphology."
"Syntax."
Etc.
And then again
An index of Latin words . . .
In the preface,
L. R. Palmer states that

<u>The Latin Language</u>
Is a book for everyone,
From specialists to laity
Who are interested in Latin
From the Bronze Age
To the Empire's fall.
He assumes no previous knowledge
Of comparative philology,
And his aim is to state
"The *communis opinio*,"
The common consensus,
And to set forth fairly
The evidence and the views
Divergent from the ones
He has expressed.
Sometimes the preface
And the table of contents
Are enough . . .
If the skeptic objects,
Let him examine page 56,
111, or 122.
Let him see pages 193 ff:
The evolution of "*pax*,"
From the end of war to
The cessation of persecution
To the peace between man and God,
Christ himself peace,
The state of the soul,
The place of eternal peace,
The peace of those who
Die in the faith,

The family of Christ,
The community of the church,
A certificate of orthodoxy,
And, too, a kiss . . .
Yes, sometimes the preface
And the table of contents
Are enough . . .
The glow one may touch
Of great scholarship,
The peace in the presence
Of which one may stand . . .
A sense of the contents
And the fairness of the author
Of which one need not read,
I.e. word for word.

28.

Kenneth Quinn, Professor of Classics
At University College, Toronto,
Editor of <u>Catullus, The Poems</u>,
St. Martin's Press, New York,
Says: "In Poem 16, C. abuses
Aurelius and Furius, his friends of Poem 11 . . ."
The first line of 16 reads as follows:
"*Pedicabo ego vos et irrumabo . . .*"
Quinn suggests in his "Commentary"
That "We may translate line 1 with Copley,
'Nuts to you, boys (i.e. Aurelius and Furius),
Nuts and go to hell.'"
Literally, however, *pedicare* means
To insert one's prick into another's asshole,
Whereas *irrumare* means
To insert one's prick into another's mouth.
Quinn admits that the literal, obscene meaning,
"Though submerged," remains available
To add to the salt and charm
Of these not enough modest
And voluptuous little poems.
One might argue whether "submerged"
Is to the point, here,
Or perhaps Quinn intends a pun.
That said, however,
It is worth noting that
The meter of 16 is hendecasyllabic,
A form introduced into Latin by Laevius

And later used by Martial, Petronius, *et al.*
It is furthermore noteworthy that
J. W. Mackail in his 1895
Edition of <u>Latin Literature</u>
Places Catullus among
The greatest lyric poets,
Alongside Sappho and Shelley . . .
Lest all you cocksuckers
And rumpfuckers forget,
Catullus rightly points out
That whereas it is proper that a poet
Be pious and pure,
His little poems need not . . .
This edition is the copyright
Of Kenneth Quinn, 1970, 1973.
All rights reserved.
No part of the publication
May be reproduced or transmitted,
In any form or by any means,
Without the editor's say so.

29.

The blurb on the second page
Of <u>Cruelty and Civilization</u>
By Roland Auguet asserts
That "the great spectacles
Of Ancient Rome were not
Merely casual entertainment,"
Not a mere choice, like the movies,
But a "public opiate,"
Which, like an air brush,
Brushed away the trifles
And highlighted the rhythm
And the shine of the Romans'
Lives and days,
The hills, the plane trees,
And the sea they called
Their own . . .
Even now, we remember
The "*bestiarius*," Carpophorus,
The charioteer, Scorpus,
And Hermes, about whom
Martial writes:
"The toast of Rome,"
The man of the century,
Skilled in all weapons, in terror,
And as Martial puts it,
Only as he can:
"No one to replace him, except himself."
How the clamor of the crowd

Clamors itself silly.
And the men behind the scenes:
The men called "*doctor*:" the trainers
Entrusted with perfecting
"The techniques of gladiators and charioteers,"
The "*editor*:" the bankroller *ludorum*,
I.e. of the games,
The masculine "*ludus*" variously translated,
"Play," "spectacle," "exhibition,"
Sometimes "pastime," "child's play," or
"Mere sport."
It is believed that
The gladiatorial combats
Were at first funerary rites
Of the upper classes,
Of the best that money could buy . . .
The belief was that
"In the end, human blood,
Spilt in honour of the dead,
Could assure a permanent revival . . ."
And, oh, yes, the longing for God,
As it were He would enter
Only through their wounds.

30.

Martial tells us that
The Porticus Vipsania,
Which stood
In the field of Mars,
Leaked,
Perhaps due to
Wear and tear,
A fault,
Its slippery stone
Perpetually wet . . .
He tells us of
A boy
Who happened
To enter under
Its dewy roof,
The moss and stain,
How he looked up,
Just at the right time
And just in the right place . . .
How an icicle
Weary of winter's ice
Fell down and pierced
His throat,
And then how
The delicate dagger
Then melted
In the heat of his wound,
As it were

A crucial instantiation
Of the indiscernibility
Of water and blood.
The last lines, 7 and 8,
Of this epigram,
I.e. Liber 4,18
Are untranslatable.
And that's how it should be
In this epigrammatic world
Where it is impossible
To figure . . .
What Fortune's up to,
How water at once
So soft and fluid
In which to swim and sail upon
Can also slit your throat.

31.

According to Fustel de Coulanges
In <u>The Ancient City</u>,
First published in 1864,
Now a Doubleday Anchor Book,
The Romans (and the Greeks, as well)
Thought of their laws as *carmina*,
I.e. "songs," "poetry,"
"Incantation," "oracles,"
Tunes of come what may and what shall be.
To change a letter, a word,
To alter the rhythm
"Was to destroy the law itself,"
"The sacred form under which
It was revealed to man . . ."
The law prayer, the voice,
Its unique quavers and keys,
The lapidary quality
And the configuration of the letters
On the tongue and page,
Not the principle,
Not the moral of the story,
But the words,
The "force . . . in the sacred words
That compose it . . ."
Words that presented
Themselves without being sought,
Words without bodily defect . . .
Thus: just as in the numbers of the days of a life

A man is obliged to devote a part
Of its full count to the gods,
So, all the cities he builds shall be eternal.
And though a man may subdue nature,
He shall be forever
Subdued by his own thoughts . . .
The cover of the Anchor Book edition
Is by Edward Gorey and so's its typography,
Printed in the U.S.A. . . .
The song is yours.

32.

It's line 312, in Book VII
Of Virgil's <u>Aeneid</u>,
"The cruel wife of Jove,"
Juno speaking . . .
She's tried everything
In the book of Gods
To prevent the Trojans
From establishing
Their Latin kingdoms . . .
But the fates are unmoved.
Lavinia, daughter
Of Latinus and Amata,
Betrothed to Turnus,
Will marry Aeneas.
At the end of Book XII
Turnus will have fled
Indignantly to the Shades below,
And Rome
Will rule the world.
Juno says: "*esto*,"
Which means "it shall be,"
Or "so be it."
Nevertheless, it's line 312,
The line to keep your eye on:
"*Flectere si nequeo Superos, Acheronta movebo.*"
Which means,
"If I (Juno) can't bend the gods above,
I will move Acheron,

I.e. the abode of the dead."
The curse of Juno is
That, yes, men will build cities,
But nothing they build will perish,
Every city nothing but
Another psychical entity
In which every phase of the past
Exists simultaneously with
Every ever-unfolding present.
Aeneas and Lavinia will dream
And their daughters and sons
Will become ghosts of wishes,
Every child from now on
A texture of associations,
A labyrinth of riddles,
A woman and man, masks,
Personae of infantile indecencies,
All our yes's yes and so, too, our no's . . .
And, of course, the secrets
None of us can keep,
The thousand or more unnoticed openings
Through which from below spills the soul.

33.

At the beginning of
Anthony Barrett's biography
Of Caligula, pages xii–xiv,
The author includes a prefatory section
Entitled, "Outline of Significant Events,"
Some of which are:
Caligula's birth, August 31, 12 A.D.,
Made *quaestor* in 33,
Meaning, administrator of finances.
In 37, hailed as *Imperator*,
Granted powers by the senate,
And then given the title *Pater Patriae*:
At the age of 25
Father of his Country . . .
And then some.
On June 10, 38, his sister, Drusilla dies.
Caligula himself dies in late January, 41,
Assassinated during the Ludi Palatini,
I.e. the Palatine Games.
Barrett writes that the "highly speculative
Dates (in the "Outline")
Are indicated by italics."
And that "the chronology of events
In Judaea in 39 and 40 is
Particularly uncertain . . ."
Again, Barrett says softly that Caligula
Had "his own ironical view of the world,"
"A highly developed sense of humour . . ."

Naturally, many of Barrett's claims
Are supported by Suetonius and Dio Cassius.
E.g. see Suetonius, The Twelve Caesars,
"Gaius (Caligula)," especially 22ff.,
"Ff.," meaning "following (pages)"
And perhaps here not inappropriately
Suggestive of "*fortissimo*," too.
Although some sense of Caligula
Can be inferred from what we have
Of Tacitus' Annals,
Unfortunately, all
Of the Caligula section
Is forever lost,
A heartbreaking lacuna of a time
Of madness for some,
Security for many,
And, as always, fun for the few.
You have to wonder about
How such words become lost . . .
(As Balsdon wondered
And lamented the loss of Agrippina's.)
Were they misplaced or forgotten?
Neglected or suppressed?
Were they erased, buried, or burned?
You have to wonder about
How could a person be so careless?
So stupid, such a fool . . .
Anyway, the character Caligula,
Who speaks Stuart Gilbert's English
Translated from Albert Camus' French
In the latter's play, Caligula, says:

"I've merely realized that
There's only one way of
Getting even with the gods.
All that's needed is
To be as cruel as they are."
Of course, the point is:
The jokes that are biggest and best
Are essentially absurd:
Both funny and not funny at all . . .
Barrett, however, quite rightly, warns
In the "Foreword" that one
Can never understand Caligula
Simply by "limiting (oneself)
Essentially to paraphrased selections
Of Suetonius and Dio."
Obviously, one should exercise
The same caution when reading Camus
And, that is, whether in English or French.

34.

Nicolas Bergier (1557–1632)
Was wrong to argue that its roads
Were built up in layers,
The metaphor borrowed from geology,
And perhaps, too, from that sense
Of *traditio*, the "handing down,"
As well as the "betrayal" of
What might have been its builders' virtue
Radiating from the center of Rome.
Grenier in <u>Archeologie gallo-romaine</u>
And Fustier in <u>La Route</u>,
1934 and '68 respectively,
Demonstrate convincingly that
The layer theory is both
Misguided and misconceived.
The point is that Bergier and his followers
Never looked carefully at the details:
The problems of building without cement,
The nature of paving stones,
Their sizes in inches
Sometimes as much as 20 by 55,
The road bed, the use of fill,
The crown, the tilt and border,
The access ramps, ruts,
The cuts through the many mountains
And the ever-sinking marsh lands.
Needham in <u>Science and Civilization in China</u>
Volume, 4, parts ii–iii suggests

The superiority of Chinese over Roman roads,
Emphasizing especially their straightness and width.
None of Needham's claims, however,
About ancient Chinese roads
Can be substantiated with hard evidence,
Since none of those Chinese roads was paved . . .
"And accordingly hardly a trace
Of their ancient roads has survived."
I.e. according to Lionel Casson's
Travel in the Ancient World,
Professor Emeritus in the classics at NYU.
Surely in this, or any, context
One might wonder about the extension
And thereby the legitimacy of
The use of the term "superiority,"
Given the fecundity of the term
"Road" itself:
The road to the stars,
The road to nowhere,
The road to my heart . . .
All the roads to Rome and of the deserts and seas . . .
The roads of the town and country,
And, of course, the road to hell . . .
The thoughts of Dean Moriarty On the Road,
Thin and blue-eyed with "a real Oklahoma accent,"
"A sideburned hero of the snowy West."
And Marylou, his pretty little blonde,
The road of Jean Louis Lebris de Kerouac,
Born March 12,1922, in Lowell, Mass.

35.

On Monday mornings
When it seems impossible
To know where
One begins and ends,
I can't help picturing
The cover of the Penguin edition
Of Livy's <u>Early History of Rome</u>,
The reverse of a silver denarius
Of the Republic, 100–97, B.C..
The denarius was worth about a dime,
And the image struck appears to be
Of four horses prancing in concert,
The profiles of their worn heads,
As it were fanned across the coin,
Two human-like figures:
The smaller of two,
A child riding bareback,
The other in his chariot,
Perhaps a victor of foreign campaign,
Now the details of his deeds
Lost in the exchange
And the rub of many hands.
Livy, in effect, says that
Even though he has "misgivings"
About writing his history,
Rome nonetheless deserves it,
And nonetheless he claims
(Somewhat disingenuously) that

If his work passes unnoticed,
He will console himself
With the greatness of his rivals,
Or closer to the original's
Literal sense,
He will console himself
"With the nobility and greatness
Of those men who will eclipse (his) name . . ."
Even though Livy knows that
The historian can never begin
At the beginning, that
The beginning, like Monday morning,
Is a fiction from which a history begins . . .
Even though he knows the paradox of history,
That in the end, like Monday morning,
History teaches us only
That it teaches us nothing at all . . .
Nevertheless, he believes,
As you and I too must believe,
That by polishing the past with words,
Exchanging all that we have
For all we can hope for,
Only then shall its details be revealed.

36.

Pliny, that is, the Elder,
Wasn't what we'd call a scientist.
He practiced what Claude
Levi-Strauss called: *bricolage*,
A kinda banging together of
The things you have at hand,
More like myth practice
Than, as I say, science.
Pliny fell into the trap
Of the illusion that
Just as daylight scares away,
I.e. distinguishes,
The natural from the synthetic
Fibers of the forced labor
Of our make-believe,
Thus, in principle,
He inferred (of course, wrongly) that
Observatio, that is, the action of watching,
Is prior to *scientia*, that is, knowledge.
Pliny didn't know that what we know
Is the result of pain, the pain
Of letting go of what we think we know
For what we now know better, even though
It's going to take time to believe.
In short, just as Pliny never knew
Claude Lévi-Strauss, author
Of <u>The Savage Mind</u>,
He also never knew Sir Karl Raimund Popper,

Author of <u>The Logic of Scientific Discovery</u>,
My edition, the Harper Torchbook,
A most distinguished series,
The dedication: "To my wife,"
The theme: *scientia et potentia refutationis*,
That is, "knowledge and the power of
The process of disproving."
Yet Pliny did know or . . .
He thought he knew the following,
Banged together by Majno, *op. cit.* 342 ff.:
Under "On the World and Physics,"
Pliny knew that "Light travels faster than sound."
He was "certain" that
"Every liquid becomes smaller when frozen."
Under "On Mankind,"
Pliny knew that
Snakes do not bite snakes,
But that most of man's evils
"Come from his fellow man,"
That "man is the only animal
For whom mating for the first time
Is followed by repugnance,"
That "civilization depends . . . on paper"
And is impossible "without salt."
Pliny knew "noble accents
And lucid, inescapable rhythms."
Under "On Doctors and Diseases,"
Pliny knew that
"The variety of diseases is unlimited."
Under "On Prodigious Events,"
Pliny knew that

"There are islands that float
And drift with the wind."

37.

First published in 1960,
Ancient Rome by Duncan Taylor
Is, as the dust cover says,
"The classic story of
The rise and fall of Rome . . ."
"Here for boys and girls . . ."
Along with 31 illustrations,
(Including a photo of
The chariot race from M.G.M.'s Ben Hur)
Maps, dates, and bibliography,
Everything in 80 pages
From the legend of Dido
To the Etruscans, Patricians, and Plebs . . .
To Marius, Cicero, and
How Crassus died . . .
From the Ides of March . . .
From the year of the four Emperors . . .
Antonius Pius, Marcus Aurelius,
And The Year 410.
From the first map, which is
Virtually empty, on page 6
To the last on page 72 now full,
The Romans move, like weather fronts,
And sweep over the Apennines and Alps,
And then as far as the Toros Daglari,
Swirling, the scent of spice
From up the Nile and around and beyond.
Surely the adolescent can easily imagine

On the page and page by page
The soldiers and their shields,
The mules, the elephants, the gore,
The trains of people and fire . . .
To the horizon,
The double duty of the young:
To kill the young and care for the old . . .
The wonder of the child himself,
The demon, the stone child of man,
The child forgotten in the last town,
Who clings to Augustus' tunic,
I.e. the Augustus of Primaporta,
Executed *circa* 20 B.C.
Taylor does well to bring to life
That long ago and far away
By citing Lord Macauley's
"Horatius," the first of
<u>The Lays of Ancient Rome</u> . . .
And he cites as well:
Shakespeare's "Coriolanus,"
Naturally, "Julius Caesar,"
Sir Walter Raleigh, A. E. Housman,
And even Noel Coward's "Operette" . . .
In the end Taylor cites
The words of an unknown poet
Who wrote in the third century A.D.:
"Cras amet, qui numquam amavit;
Quique amavit, cras amet!"
Meaning: "Let him love tomorrow, who has never loved;
And who has loved, tomorrow let him love!"
Perhaps a good place to end

"For boys and girls,"
But on second thought, perhaps not.
See, it's "tomorrow" that's so troublesome . . .
Is it substantive or merely an adverb?
Meaning: on the day after today?
Or meaning: the day that will never arrive?

38

201 Latin Verbs
by Joseph Wohlberg
Published by
The Barron's Educational Series, Inc.
Contains the most often found verbs
Fully conjugated in all tenses
And alphabetically arranged.
You'll find not only
Canere, capere, clamare, and *cupire,*
I.e. to sing, to seize, to shout, and wish,
But also *patere,* to lie open,
Superare, to overcome,
Videre, to see,
And *vigilare,* to watch . . .
As in all through the night.
Wohlberg explains precisely
How to translate from Latin to English
Voice for voice, mood for mood,
Person for person, number for number . . .
And tense for tense.
The active, the passive,
The indicative, the subjunctive,
The infinitive, its present, perfect, and future,
And finally the command.
He shows clearly
How the imperfect is imperfect
In the sense of "I was carrying"
As opposed to the perfect,

"I carried" and that was that.
Without any acknowledgements of
The contradictions therein
He discusses the present's senses
Of "am" and "do,"
Without remorse the pluperfect
And non-dogmatically how
Every future will be perfect, too,
Whether we like it or not.
It's a sad book Wohlberg writes,
Sad in so far as it is
A tragedy or a comedy, and perhaps both.
It's our inflections, how
We join ourselves together . . .
It's our simple and compound forms,
Their finite variations,
The recursive sense of ourselves,
Boxes within boxes,
Which generate infinite times, such as:
Of that day I walked.
The way we held and knew.
And when you will promise
Or never forget . . .
Promise, cross your heart . . .
How one can return
While the other still waits,
And neither will ever see . . .
It's all about existence, shade, and color,
Overtones of wish, obligation,
Possibility and idea,
And then how all

You've ever thought about
Bang! can be washed away,
And yet it's all about
Just the dazzle and lo! of it all . . .
Of when someone long ago said
"*Possum*" and we know
Now it means "I can."

39.

Homages are footnotes,
Or at least not unlike footnotes,
Except the homage is composed
Without respect either to
The style of or the law of
God, gods, Chicago, or MLA.
The homage allows that you say anything
You want,
Feign humility without being humiliating . . .
Wear any disguise you choose,
Talk of the "Light, light of (your) eyes . . ."
"Expound the distensions of Empires,"
Hack out pictures such as:
". . . hung here, a scare-crow of lovers."
Or worse yet:
"The Muses clinging to the mossy ridges . . ."
Or "she will sit before your feet in a veil . . ."
And after you're dead,
The critics will say, of course,
That although you wrote
Your own reviews,
You never merely translated
Something into something,
What was into what is.
Rather you invented the future.
Hence endowing the future perfect
With an existence all of its own.
In the 6th elegy of "Book IV" of the <u>Elegies</u>

Edited by W. A. Camps,
Arno Press, A New York Times Company,
New York, 1979,
Sextus Propertius writes
"*Sacra facit vates: sint ora faventia sacris*
et cadat ante meos icta iuuenca focos."
Which may be translated
"The poet-priest is performing the rites of the Muses.
Favour with silence. A heifer must fall at the shrine."
I prefer to risk stating flat out,
(Even though "*facit*" is ambiguous)
"The poet makes sacred things."
Since "to make" has that creative sense,
Which "to perform" might lack.
Also I would flesh out the sense of "*sint . . .*"
That subjunctive sense of
Letting our mouths be favorable to sacred things,
And at the same time suggesting that "favorable"
Here implies silence.
By the way, that ain't fuckin' easy.
Of course, I would continue to maintain
The subjunctive and dispose entirely
Of the falsely apodictic "must fall."
Clearly Propertius' second line should read:
"And may the stuck heifer fall before my hearth."
By the way, Langenscheidt's Pocket
Defines "*iuuenca*" as "young woman," too.
Given Propertius' rough track record in love,
That's interesting.
Also, "*cado*" means not only "fall,"
But "drop," "be killed," and "cease," as well.

86

Also, the 6th elegy might be thought of
As the poet humbling himself before
The acts of the emperor . . .
The acts of the latter a conquest of space,
The poet who conquers time.

40.

Of all the books in all the libraries
In all the basements in all the attics
And under all the beds,
The footnotes in Gelzer's
Caesar, Harvard UP,
Cambridge, Mass.,
Are among the most elegant
In the sense of polished and pure
As well as rich
In the sense of resonant and big.
Here is the page, page after page
Crafted to perfection,
The equilibrium of the text maintained
By the circulation of its notes
Intending toward their respective sources,
The metaphor clearly suggesting
The text as body and as body
Its insatiable desire for food . . .
The abbreviations, the lilting italics,
The limpid numbers of the chapters and lines,
The sources of yesterday,
And, of course, of long ago.
Without Caesar in the world,
One might falsely hold that
The act of reading is lacking
In the values of touch,
How all art aspires to the condition of touch . . .
The line, the light and the dark,

Color, pictorial space, unity and materials,
The flat surface, and motion and time . . .
How the note at the bottom of the page
Places the body in the world . . .
How when the parts have been counted
And accounted for,
The whole is always greater.
On page 139, Gelzer writes
That in the early summer of 54
On a journey from northern Italy
To yet another scene of military travail,
Caesar composed a grammatical work,
The now lost <u>De Analogia</u>.
In it, he recommends that
The forms of grammatical inflection
Should be chosen according to reason,
The aim being simplicity, clarity, etc.
"As the sailor avoids the rock,
So, should you the obsolete and rare word."
Gelzer says: "The same motto could
Just as well be applied to [Caesar's] policies . . ."
A man whose genius,
Which does not exclude a desire for
Its own destruction and the simplicity thereof,
Lay in his ability
"To imbue others with his own intentions
And with their help to increase
The effectiveness of the weapons
Which determine the very nature of the world."

41.

Theodor Mommsen's <u>The History of Rome:</u>
<u>An account of the events and people</u>
<u>From the conquest of Carthage</u>
<u>To the end of the Republic</u>
Came out in a "new edition" in 1958.
In the Intro. the editors, Saunders and Collins,
Tell the reader "The plan of this work."
They explain that they want to revive
The attention that Mommsen's work
Had deservedly received in Mark Twain's time . . .
That work on the Republic,
Which was fading into "limbo"
When the last English edition,
The four volume Everyman, went out of print,
And municipal libraries mercilessly
Began stamping it "discard."
<u>The History of Rome</u>, its 2,000 pages plus,
Rather than being read was becoming
Dusted with and desiccated by admiration and respect.
Hence the plan of a one-volume work . . .
A work intended for "non-specialists."
Given that all Roman history before 250 B.C.
Is speculative at best,
Saunders and Collins concluded it safe to
Cut the first third of the <u>History</u>,
As well as "the very important, exciting,
And well-documented 100 years from 250 to 150,"
When Rome beat Carthage three nothing,

And then went on to pacify the Hellenic world.
They also eliminated chapters on
Art, religion, and culture, "which do not always
Sustain the excellence of . . ."
Political and military affairs.
They left out the campaigns in the East and in Gaul,
Deleting unfamiliar Roman words and phrases,
As well as obscure allusions to
The recent and far away past . . .
So, the "new edition" runs 588 pages,
Approximately one quarter of the original 2000 plus.
Perhaps it should be noted that the <u>OLD</u>,
Defines the word "*specialis*" as
"Particular as opposed to general,
Specific, individual, having
The nature of *species*, i.e.
Something presented to view, a spectacle, a sight,
A look, a surface film given off by physical objects,
A pomp, a show, a vision, or form,
The details of the nature of a species."
Perhaps also it should be noted that Saunders and
    Collins
Reworked the Dickson translation,
That is, Dr. William P. Dickson
Professor of Divinity at the University of Glasgow,
Changing the paragraphing, punctuation,
Chopping down the sentences, re-structuring,
Polishing the uneven edges,
Omitting the colloquial and archaic phrases
And substituting in their place the modern expressions
We can all understand . . .

The "specialist," according to <u>Webster's</u>,
Is "one who devotes himself to a special occupation,"
"Special" meaning "distinguished by some unusual
    quality,"
"Peculiar," or better yet, "unique."

42.

You might think that
Footnotes are fundamentally
Content driven,
Things that should be added to,
Things that should be remembered about,
Lines that in an innocent age
Would have stood by themselves.
But innocence, if it ever existed at all,
Is *sua natura*, i.e. by its own nature,
Of a condition that is
Beyond the bounds of recall . . .
Footnotes are the lines
Between the lines between lines *ad infinitum*
Et sub specie aeternitatis, too,
That is, infinitely and from forever.
The footnote endows every word with
An explanation and justification . . .
Say, how one might come to understand
How one might dedicate a life
To understanding each line, word by word,
How each word may be a spirit *in se*,
I.e. in itself or just
The bottom line of a tree
Of directories and subdirectories
And switches on and off . . .
How important it is to understand
That in Book II, chapter 38, line 6
In Tacitus' <u>Annales</u>

"*Augeamus*," which means "we increase,"
Should, according to Furneaux, be taken
By zeugma with "*negotia*," meaning "businesses,"
"Zeugma" that lovely rhetorical figure,
Which uses one word to modify
Or to govern two or more words,
Hence the line:
"*Ut privata negotia et*
Res familiares nostras
Hic augeamus."
That is: "so that we increase
Our private businesses
And our family stuff,"
"We increase" aiming ever so nicely
At "businesses" and "stuff," double barrel . . .
How it is also crucial to know
That "*intendetur*" in the same chapter
Means "will be aggravated,"
And, again, according to Furneaux,
That "sense of the word . . .
Almost [entirely] Tacitean,"
The power of a man
To make a word, and
Not only to make meaning,
But to make it with his name on it . . .
To make it his.
Yes, it's the infinite,
And how we make it . . .
The quest for the forms
Of the language of content,
The footnotes of the way you walk,

The way you sleep and put food in . . .
The arms from one body that go around
Another body snake-like and almost zeugma-wise,
Their fingers' tips reading Braille and likewise
The moves of the lines between the lines,
That all knowledge is the knowledge of architecture:
The knowledge that nothing exists
Strong enough to stand on its own.

43.

In note 1 on chapter XXI, line 2,
Editors Gould and Whiteley write
That in chapter IX, Laelius said:
". . . *verae amicitiae sempiternae sunt*,"
Meaning "true friendships are everlasting,"
"*Sempiternae*" the feminine nominative plural
Formed from "*semper*" and the suffix "*-erna*,"
The latter indicating the "the enlargement of,"
The former, "always."
The reason why true friendships are everlasting
Is that nature cannot change when a friend is true,
A point which is re-enforced by the repercussion
Of the Latin diphthong's "-ae," sounding "I," "I,"
   "I" . . .
When I was a boy like other boys,
I threw stones into the river.
I admired the concentric forms they formed . . .
How they grew and intersected . . .
How they seemed to spin . . .
And how I called them mine . . .
And how thereby, too, I could look in
And out at the same time.
All the non-discursive night missives
I sent out to myself
And dreamed of sending to you . . .
But for the fear
Of whether or not
Or what

You might reply.
I know I've read somewhere
That we all have the need
To forge for ourselves
An image of what exists,
That we need to externalize that image,
And so duplicate ourselves for ourselves,
With the result that one can see oneself
By oneself and then both in and through another,
As it were all together: alone, in the river,
And through the face of another man . . .
In the beginning of chapter XXI
Cicero points out that, of course,
Not all friendships are true.
There exist the friendships of wise men
And the friendships of the vulgar, as well.

44.

In chapter 28 of
<u>The Oxford History of the Classical World</u>,
Richard Jenkyns writes
Of silver Latin's poetry and prose,
Pictures including
A woman from Roman Egypt,
A cup of a dance of skulls,
The worship of Isis
From the Herculaneum's walls . . .
Thoughts of pleasure and jewels,
Death, and the hope of a life forever more.
At the end of the chapter,
Under "Further Reading,"
Jenkyns suggests that you consult
At least some of the following:
Arrowsmith's translation of <u>The Satyricon</u>,
Ann Arbor, 1962,
Michie's Martial, Green's Juvenal,
As well as Dryden's renderings
In <u>The Poems of John Dryden</u>,
Edited by J. Kinsley, Oxford, 1958.
Jenkyns also suggests that
You compare Samuel Johnson's "imitations"
Of Juvenal's <u>Satires</u> 3 and 10,
Which he entitled "London"
And "The Vanity of Human Wishes,"
And compare, too, Walter Pater's
Translation of Apuleius' <u>Cupid and Psyche</u>

Included in chapter 5 of his <u>Marius the Epicurean</u>,
A translation that "conveys
Something of Apuleius' elegance,
Though not of his verve."
G. Williams' <u>Change and Decline:</u>
<u>Roman Literature in the Early Empire</u>
Surveys the whole period,
While others are aimed
At the interests of the specialist,
Others such as,
<u>Persius and the Programmatic Satire:</u>
<u>A Study in Form and Imagery,</u>
And "Is Juvenal a classic?"
In <u>Critical Essays on Roman Literature</u>:
There are pictures of women, silver, and then
More thoughts of pleasure and of forever,
Further reading: the minds of Michie,
Dryden, Johnson . . . Green,
And further reading: Perry's
<u>The Ancient Romances:</u>
<u>A Literary-Historical Account of their Origins</u>,
Berkeley, 1967 . . .

45.

Contrary to what is implied in n. 42,
The footnote is not merely
A reading between the lines, and so on,
But also a *writing* between the lines,
The intent of the writer
To fill up the vacuum,
No matter how tight the spaces, which,
We are taught, nature so abhors.
G. W. Bowersock, Professor of Ancient History
At the Institute for Advanced Study at Princeton,
Gibbon scholar and author of
Julian the Apostate, Roman Arabia, and others,
Characterizes the footnote as "free,"
"Connected," but "stand[ing] above,"
A take, like a Coltrane take,
The taker, an author of "pensees or aphorisms,"
Characteristic of the thought of any man,
Appearing both bound to the earth
And unbound at the same time.
Gibbon, according to Bowersock, simply
Thought the footnote a subtext,
The club of the text,
The blunt clout enhanced
To intimidate further and to persuade . . .
Or perhaps in a more delicate respect,
"A kind of counterpoint with [*sic*] the text,"
Or perhaps in a text-less universe, i.e.
In the absence or extinction of text,

A counterpoint to nothing . . .
Or with nothing but yourself.
There's no doubt about it,
The aspiring footnoter, as Bowersock says,
Despairs at the foot of Gibbon's throne.
And he's right, too, when he says,
How the footnote allows the writer
To be more relaxed and conversational
And allows him to expose his quirky side,
The horror at the corner of every smile,
That side, which one is so reluctant to divulge
    elsewhere,
"A kind of note at the foot of the last page . . ."
That corner, which adapts so well to that
Finer print sense of ourselves.

46.

It is worth noting in
The Classics: a Journal of Greek and Latin
Philosophy, History, and Literature,
Volume XXIII, #1, Spring, 1963,
The article audaciously entitled
"Out of Breath: A Brief Examination
Of the Self-Execution of Petronius 'Arbiter',"
The author: Howard V. Kipnis,
Assistant Professor in the Humanities Dept.,
Cape Cod Community College, Hyannis Port, Mass.
The well-known event to which Kipnis refers,
Of course, is the death of Petronius at Cumae.
Like many others under the empire, Petronius,
Too, had been arrested on false charges.
He decided that rather than endure
The indignities of red tape,
He would open a vein, probably
The radial or ulnar . . .
Even though we'll never know for sure.
Now and then he would squeeze off the flow,
Talk with his friends, nothing serious,
No philosophy, no discourses on
The immortality of the soul, etc.
Just a few songs . . .
At one point he gave some of his slaves presents,
A modest expression of his gratitude . . .
Others he beat.
Finally, he appeared at dinner,

And as it were fell asleep.
Kipnis takes the story from Tacitus.
However, the story is but a means to his point.
After consulting Cicero, Lucretius, Seneca, *et al.*,
Including the character Trimalchio of the famous
    "*Cena*,"
Meaning "Dinner," or more specifically here "Dinner
    Party,"
Kipnis makes a case for the significance
Of distinguishing the sudden from
The slow death in Roman culture,
And what it, i.e. the distinction, implies.
Although the sudden death has the advantages
Of not letting the victim, i.e. the *delectus*,
Meaning the man "chosen," "picked," or "removed,"
Know what hit him,
It precludes the man who has both
Wit and composure from both
Assessing and contemplating
The time of his own "life-scape,"
"Life-scape" a neologism, according to Kipnis,
Which appears only in the Satyricon,
Which, however, I might add,
Is not supported by the <u>OLD</u>.
In any case, it seems that the gods allow,
As a final favor, the slow death
Only to those of us who are capable
Of poetic faith, i.e. in the Coleridge sense
Of suspending disbelief in
The history of one's own life,
Of appreciating with good humor and grace

That one is neither conqueror nor conquered,
Even though it is without doubt
Some slaves deserve the beating they get . . .
Kipnis also points out in a footnote that Petronius
    "Arbiter"
May be the same person as Titus Petronius Niger,
Who was not only arbiter of elegance
But also *consul suffectus*, i.e. a substitute consul, 62
    A.D.

47.

"An Unsolved Problem of Historical Forgery:
The *Sciptores Historiae Augustae*,"
That is, The Writers of Augustan History,
By Arnaldo Momigliano
First appeared in
The Journal of the Warburg and Courtauld Institutes,
1954,
And later was included in
Studies in Historiography, Harper & Row,
An edition which also includes
Gibbon's contribution to historical method.
Momigliano, teacher of,
Among others, Anthony Grafton,
Claims that the Historia Augusta
Is not a Christian document,
Rather one of a dying paganism,
A subtle distinction,
But not on that account
Any less clear . . .
That having been said,
M. urges that the modern reader
Keep in mind, what he quaintly refers to as,
"The unstable standards of honesty
Of the late Greek and Roman writers."
Indeed, Athanasius was accused
Of systematic forgery of documents,
That very same Athanasius, the saint, who argued
That Christ was identical in substance

Or co-essential with the Father, hence truly God.
M. also mentions that <u>The Life of Constantine</u>
By Eusebius is still the object of heated debate,
Concerning both its authenticity as a whole
And the authenticity of the documents
Which purportedly support it . . .
As you might expect, discussion about
The truth of the Acts of the Martyrs
Still rages on.
But it is not the forgery,
The scholarly sleight of hand itself
That interests a man such as Momigliano.
For he clearly states:
"Even when we are certain of the forgery,
It is sometimes difficult for us
To understand the forger's mind."
Perhaps he's a propagandist.
Perhaps he just loves a joke.
How can you figure, for example,
What's what in the mind of the man
Who cooks up the correspondence
Between Seneca and St. Paul?
A correspondence, according to M.,
Concocted in the fourth century A.D.,
The content of which is trivial
And whose style is effete.
Call it a correspondence,
But, in fact, M. concludes:
"A mixture of naivety, vulgarity,
And pedantry for the sake of
What tries to pretend to be art . . ."

And yet the motives of which
Are difficult, if not impossible, to comprehend.
Surely forgeries express the *Weltanschauung*
Of the forger, that is, his "world view."
However, as M. rightly points out,
"There remains a difference between the
    Weltanschauung
Of the man who wants to conceal his identity,
And the [one] of the man who does not."
With all due respect to Momigliano,
He does not make it at all clear
What precisely that difference is,
And whether the difference is one
Of degree or a difference in kind.

48.

It's not the rhyme that counts,
It's the corporeal metronome
Of our words' ticks,
Which measure (not determine)
The pseudo poem, in the sense
Of aspiring towards Perfect-hood,
An Ideal, *sui generis*, which by definition
Of its uppercase character,
Is beyond the bounds of
The merely real . . .
The word, like the moment,
Is a slave to mortality,
And so, too, the strings of them,
No matter how seductive
The lick of any footnote might be,
I mean, of course, "lick" in that
Jazzy *lingere* sense of the word,
I.e. big and juicy . . .
Ya see, Hadrian, *loc. cit.*
Meaning *loco citato*,
I.e. "in the place cited,"
Was never understood,
Neither by Spartianus or Yourcenar,
Nor by his boyfriend or his wife.
The given for Hadrian
Was the terse quality of the earth,
Its elliptical expressions,
The half-life forms the earth formed,

The breaks in their lines
Which defied, except temporarily,
Any statement of a set of rules.
For Hadrian it was never merely
The banal question, the questions of metaphysics:
What's light? What's soul? What's body? What's dark?
It was never a question of what's said, the song.
What Hadrian wanted to know
(And this is what S. and Y. missed)
Was where the accidents of earth,
Such as body and soul, meet,
And how and when and why?
Had Hadrian lived today
He would have been a film maker,
Who, like the footnoter,
Appreciates the collaborative
And the derivative nature of things,
I.e. knowing everything is but half-baked,
Who aspires beyond time to . . . whaddayacallit . . .
And simultaneously knowing
The deadlines and the money-men preclude
The possibility of complete success.

49.

One reason for writing footnotes is Gibbon's,
According to Anthony Grafton, and, that is,
To piss off your enemies and amuse your friends,
And if you're particularly magnanimous,
To piss off your friends and amuse your enemies, too.
And that, of course, leads to the question why
A text at all, especially
When you can compose notes
Like Gibbon's and Grafton's
Which, who knows, may in time evolve into
A text-like species and so cry out for notes . . .
Notes of notes, generations as it were,
The survival of the fittest footnotes,
And so forth and so on.
The note gives the word its authority.
The word not only articulates problems,
Tells stories, and constructs its tedious sorites,
It also must examine the sources of its voice,
The timbre of its androgynous character,
The very nature of the voice itself,
And its peculiar registers, as well.
The note is the salt of a labor,
The blurred brought into focus,
The mumbled made into a well-formed form.
In certain apposite cases, the note
Resonates the ring of the musical note
Both in its pitch and beat.
It suggests that one's nose is up to going anywhere,

That the issues are not personal,
That the credentials one has accumulated
Are perfectly legitimate and deserve
All the hosannas and scrapings they receive.
The footnote suggests that the next guy
Can be just plain wrong, and here's the proof:
We've done the measurements and run the numbers
Once and for all, case closed . . .
And yet Grafton says in <u>The Footnote: A Curious
    History,</u>
Harvard University Press, 1997: "Once the historian
    writes
With footnotes, historical narrative tells
A distinctively modern, double story."
Of course, if you think about it, all writing is
    historical.
However, that having been said, the double story
    is this:
All words and their works aspire to "universal validity,"
The Beautiful, The Good, and The True.
And yet at the same time all words are contingent,
"Dependent on forms of research, opportunities,
States of particular questions that existed,"
When the worker happened to wake up that morning
And when, finally, and with whom he went to bed.
In the chapter entitled "Ranke's Path to the
    Footnote,"
I.e. Leopold von Ranke, the nineteenth-century
    historian
Who sought to recapture the past as it really was,
Grafton points out that Gottfried Hermann

"Raised the general questions about historical
    method . . .
About the quality and extent of the knowledge
One can hope to obtain about the past."
He told his students in an odd nineteenth-century
    German Latin:
"*Quae nobis restant graecae poeseos monumenta,*
Rudera sunt ex magno naufragio servata."
Which Grafton translates:
"The monuments of Greek poetry
That remain to us are wreckage
Saved from the broken ships
Lost to the sea."
The point being that
What passes as real ancient poetry,
I.e. prior to translation,
Is not the real item at all.
There's a paradox ready to strike here:
The note both supports and subverts
And aims at the contingent and necessary,
Then guarantees everything, i.e. in itself,
And nothing at all.
But as Gibbon said, maybe it's all about
Payback time for enemies and laughs for friends . . .
Again, Grafton cites Gibbon who cites the "learned
    Origen,"
Early Christian "philosopher" who thought
That the sure way to "disarm the tempter"
Was for the tempter himself to cut off his own balls,
Origen's point being that there's a little tempter
That lives in all of us, but especially in men.

112

Gibbon's footnote, here, is:

"As it was [Origen's] general practice
To allegorize scripture;
It seems unfortunate that, in this instance only,
He should have adopted the literal sense."
That's in chapter 15 of the <u>Decline and Fall</u>.
Grafton correctly suggests that for further
Recent information about Origen's bright idea,
One see <u>The Body and Society</u>, New York,
1988, page 168, n. 4. by Peter Brown.

50.

When you gotta look at
Inscriptions, law codes,
Ancient monuments, and letters
To make sense of it all,
As well as archaeological materials,
Formal histories, treatises,
Orations, papyri, and verse,
It shouldn't surprise anyone
That chapters in a book entitled
<u>In the Twilight of Antiquity</u>,
I.e. by Tom B. Jones,
Might seem to the reader
"Formless and without plan."
In the twilight of any day,
The emphasis is always on
Tint and hue (see n.20) rather than
On what fits and what not,
On mood rather than
On distinctions, developments,
Entelechies, the questions
Of what'll we do if we fail,
Or more difficult yet,
Of what'll we do if we get
Everything we want.
The twilight is a back light . . .
By which you're not meant to see too much,
A flat time of neither full body nor blood.
A time of cameos, mere vehicles,

During which the canvas
Becomes the projector of light
And the details upon it ciphers,
Which may suggest that as a light dies
It is only then truly that it comes alive . . .
As usual, you can never know
Whether we're talkin' here,
A gimmick or a sign . . .
But look, at least you can know this:
1. Palladas, "The Soldier and the Grammarian,"
    Seems to have been born in Eygpt about 350;
2. Contrary to what St. Jerome's letters say,
    See especially letter XXII,
    High society in fourth-century Rome
    Was not all that bad;
3. During the pilgrimage of the Holy Paula,
    She, Paula, visited the tomb of John the Baptist,
    In which she saw demons,
    Men who howled like wolves,
    The voices of dogs,
    And other men who roared like lions.
    She saw men bent over backwards,
    The tops of their heads to the ground,
    And women hung by their feet,
    Their faces covered by their clothes,
    Their assholes and what not,
    As suggested by Peregrinatio, XVI,
    As it were throwing pungent
    Kisses to the stars,
    I.e. Peregrinatio Sanctae Paulae,
    edited by T. Tobler, Geneva, 1879.

Jones points out that "pilgrim,"
Itself is the paradigm twilight term:
Etymologically a "wayfarer," a "traveler,"
A "sojourner," a "bird of passage,"
"A man or a woman from out of town . . ."
And like the chapters in a book
Entitled <u>In the Twilight of Antiquity</u>,
The twilights of pilgrims
Are without form or plan.

51.

If you're going to write
About the Roman soldier,
You'll have to take a look
At Vegetius' <u>De re militari</u>,
Which means literally
<u>About the Soldier Thing</u>
Or perhaps <u>The War Thing</u>
Depending upon how you
Construe "*militari*,"
The third declension ablative
Of the adjective, "*militaris*."
Of course, you don't even
Want to think about *res*,
Which the <u>OLD</u>
Assigns more than 50 ways to mean . . .
What's crucial, however,
But not easy,
Given Vegetius' work to be
One of a kind,
Is pinning down its
Date of composition.
G. R. Watson in <u>The Roman Soldier</u>
Estimates 383 to 395 A.D.
At the same time, Watson says:
Although Vegetius is all we've got, he
"Was neither a historian nor a soldier,"
He was a name dropper,
A mere compiler

Of "congeries of inconsistencies," etc. . . .
Like all writers of war
At all times,
V. considers, too,
The soldier's basic training:
The running, the jumping,
The swimming, the heavy packs
They bore and
"The Things They Carried" . . .
And later then
The faces on the columns
In the history books,
The short stories, the novels,
The plays of the film and stage . . .
Of loss, of triumphal processions
And arches and the insatiable
Hope of gain.

52.

Op. cit. <u>Historia Augusta</u>, p. 85,
In the Penguin Books edition,
The editors of which prefer the title:
<u>The Lives of the Later Caesars,</u>
The author of the Hadrian biography,
Presumably Aelius Spartianus,
Says the dying Hadrian composed the following verses:
"Little charmer, wanderer, little sprite,
Body's companion and guest,
To what places now will you take flight,
Forbidding and empty and dim as night?
And you won't make your wonted jest!"
Notwithstanding the awkward juxtaposition
Of "won't" and "wonted"
Anthony Birley's rhyme driven translation
Fails to capture the terse quality of
The original: "*Animula, vagula, blandula,*
Hospes comesque corporis,
Quae nunc abibis in loca
Pallidula, rigida, nudula,
Nec, ut soles, dabis iocos."
An alternative, albeit imperfect, rendition
Might be: "Little soul, wanderer, charmer,
The body's companion and guest,
You who now will go away into places:
Pale, stiff, bare . . . you,
The places one and together, now . . .

And no more jokes
To play or tell."
It should be pointed out that the suffix "u-l-a"
Acts as a diminutive in Latin,
So that the soul in Hadrian's poem,
As well as the pale places to which it is bound,
Should be construed as small and cute.
Furthermore, the suggested ambiguity
Of *pallidula*, *rigida*, *nudula*, should be noted,
Since they are clearly on the one hand
Neuter plural accusatives
Referring to *loca*, i.e. places,
And yet on the other hand point to
That nominative singular sense of the soul.
Spartianus claims that Hadrian wrote other verses
Both in Latin and in Greek, none of which were great.
Perhaps Spartianus does not think highly
Of Hadrian's verses because
Of his (i.e. Hadrian's) failure
To depict the soul . . .
However, Spartianus does not understand,
As Marguerite Yourcenar does,
That it's the body that's Hadrian's concern,
The soul a mere guest . . .
As Hadrian says in his <u>Memoirs</u>,
Farrar, Straus, & Young, p. 14,
"I have sometimes thought of constructing
A system of human knowledge which would be
Based on eroticism,
A theory of contact wherein the mysterious
Value of each being is to offer to us

Just that point of perspective
Which another world affords."
Finally, you should know that
Before Hadrian died he made sure that,
At least, some of his enemies would not outlive him,
Among them, Servianus, who was then 90 years old.

53.

Sometimes you have to quote in full
Etc. etc., as already suggested
Above, especially footnote 22 . . .
This time it's St. Augustine, <u>The Confessions</u>,
Book X, chapter 30,
In regno temporis, i.e. in the realm of time,
The Bishop of Hippo,
In aeternitate, the Saint . . .
He's talking how God
Has ordered him to restrain himself
From the concupiscence of the flesh, the eyes,
And the ambition of the world,
I.e. citing 1 John, II, 16.
God said: That's it! Enough!
No more fuckin' around.
And though He didn't say no to marriage,
He suggested a better way to go.
And so through God's grace,
Augustine became *dispensor* of the sacrament.
You would think so far so good.
But not true . . .
"*Sed adhuc vivunt in memoria mea,*
De qua multa locutus sum,
Talium rerum imagines,
Quas ibi consuetudo mea fixit;
Et occursantur mihi vigilanti
Quidem carentes viribus,
In somnis autem non solum usque

Ad delectionem sed etiam usque
Ad consensionem factumque simillimum.
Et tantum valet imaginis illius inlusio
In anima mea in carne mea,
Ut dormienti falsa visa persuadeant
Quod vigilanti vera non possunt."

Meaning:

"But even now many things live in my memory,
About which I have spoken,
The images of such things,
Which my habit fixed there (i.e. in memory);
They even occur to me while I'm awake
Though they are lacking in power.
However, in sleep they come not only continually
To my delight but also they come continually
By my consent, a virtual reality
As it were the dirty deed done.
And the illusion of that image is so great
In my soul in my flesh
That false visions persuade me sleeping
While true things cannot persuade me when I'm
   awake."

It may not be the most elegant translation,
But it's as clean as it gets.
But more important, imagine:
False things, i.e. images *qua* images,
Have greater power over sleeping men
Than true things have over them wide awake.
Augustine does not pursue whether or not
False things might imply true things.
Rather he asks: Am I not myself when I sleep?

Is there so much difference between
Myself and myself awake and sleeping?
As already suggested, the translation here is my own.
However, it is not without the influence
Of Watts (1590?–1649), rector of St. Albans,
Wood Street, London, his translation published 1631.
The Latin text is Knoll's (Teubner, 1909).

54.

Nothing can escape taking a beating,
Not even the Pantheon,
Temple of All the Gods,
The most celebrated of Agrippa's works,
I.e. Marcus Vipsanius Agrippa (63–12 B.C.),
Commander of the fleet at Actium,
Life-long friend to Augustus,
Rich, as many others, from the property
Of his political foes . . .
No one knows for sure
How much of the present building
Is Agrippa's own or even how
It might have originally appeared.
The Pantheon suffered damage by fire
In the reign of Titus,
Was repaired in the reign of Domitian,
Fire again under Trajan,
And then re-fashioned under Hadrian in the 120s.
It was further repaired by Septimius Severus
And his son Caracalla, who murdered his brother, Geta,
Who was reputed to have said:
"No one should have money except me . . ."
Whose famous Edict of 212 conferred
Roman citizenship on all inhabitants of the empire,
And then himself was murdered in 217.
In 608 the Pantheon was turned into a Christian
    church,
Abandoned now by all but one god.

The Byzantine emperor Constans II
Stripped the building of its gold-plated tiles,
And during the middle ages the marble facings were
robbed,
The statues in the niches of the rotunda already long
gone.
Finally, in 1625, Pope Urban VIII, i.e. Maffeo
Barberini,
Dismantled the Pantheon's bronze girders
In order to re-cast them into the cannon of war . . .
Contemporary opinion was divided on the Pope's
resolve.
Some said: "*Quod non fecerunt barbari fecerunt
Barberini.*"
That is: "What the barbarians didn't do the Barberini
did."
Others said: "Better that such noble material should
keep off
The enemies of the Church rather than the rain."
In any case, no one knows for sure whether
The bronze was original or was later installed by
Hadrian . . .
The front of the portico, at least, may be original.
It still bears the inscription:
*M * AGRIPPA * L * F * COS * TERTIUM * FECIT*,
meaning,
"Marcus Agrippa son of Lucius in his third consulship
made (this)."
Agrippa also furnished Nimes in Provence
With the temple now known as Maison Carre or
Square House,

And the celebrated aqueduct, Pont du Garde,
The latter a symbol for our thirst
For water and other things unknown,
The former a symbol for order and freedom
And the knowledge that both acts of good and evil
Obscure the intent of our original designs.

55.

The "Selected Readings"
At the end of <u>Love in the Ancient World</u>
Includes the following titles:
"The Eternal Triangle, First Century B.C.,"
<u>Poets in a Landscape</u>,
<u>Sexual Life in Ancient Rome</u>,
<u>Goddesses, Whores, Wives and Slaves</u>,
"The Threshold of the Self is but an Imaginary
    Line,"
"The Silent Women of Rome,"
<u>The Latin Love Elegy</u>,
And "Le Mariage des filles impuberes dans la Rome
    Antique,"
In the <u>Revue des Etudes Latines</u> (1970), 17–25,
I.e. "The Marriage of Prepubescent Girls in Ancient
    Rome."
This, of course, is not a complete list.
However, it is sufficiently tantalizing, indeed.
And that is all that is intended,
Since everyone knows, or if not, should know,
That such lists *sua natura*
Are inexhaustible . . .
As already suggested in footnote 44.
Thus, one can only imagine, and should imagine:
The Bacchanalian action at the foot of the Aventine
In the sacred grove of the Roman divinity Stimula;
The bride who begins her new life
By offering three coins, one to her husband,

One to the gods of the hearth,
And the third to the gods
Of the crossroads nearest to home.
One can only imagine . . .
The supplicant lover's
Song before the closed door,
The object of showgirls' ridicule,
His lament, his perseverance,
In Greece, the song itself already
A literary genre, viz. *paraklausithyron* . . .
And then again behind closed doors . . .
The "loves" of Augustus motivated not by passion
But in order to learn the secrets
Of the husbands whose wives he rode.
Augustus knew that the way
Into a woman's shorts
Was by deluding her into
Thinking you admired her thoughts . . .
He knew, so well,
That no woman could ever love
A man who wanted nothing less . . .
Than the world.
But the question, of course, is:
What list of secrets was he looking for?
Which then suggests, at least,
Three more questions:
By what criteria did Augustus choose what to read?
What secrets about whom?
And why do we want to know?

56.

Gibbon points out that
Diocletian had raised himself
From servile origins to the throne.
His was a time (i.e. early fourth century A.D.)
When the Empire's business was brisk,
While unfortunately the arts
Suffered yet their further decline,
The advance of the latter spelled out
In the bloodshot lines
And planes of the Empire's facades.
As Gibbon explicitly states, in Vol. 1, page 381,
If such was the state of architecture,
"The practice of architecture directed
By a few general and even mechanical rules . . ."
Then you can well imagine
Where sculpture and painting were at.
Since whereas, like architecture,
Painting and sculpture imitate nature's forms,
Unlike architecture, they imitate also
"The characters and passions of the human soul,"
Which possess neither line nor plane,
Only waves and shades of only heat and cold.
Hence the steady hand is of little avail
When it comes to the "sublime arts,"
Unless it embodies all the hands of all the phyla
And then, too, is guided by correct observation and
    taste,
The sublime arts, in principle, no different from

The arts of the fortune tellers
Who shape guts into words on a slab of stone.
Although the cash registers were ringing,
The soldiers lacked the soldier's discipline,
The flow of barbarians seemed to gush,
The progress of despotism was evermore a success . . .
None of which inspired a love for letters,
And "even the mind of Diocletian,
However active and capacious in business,
Was totally uninformed by study"
Or the simple and innocent pleasures thereof.
You see the problem with doing too much business
("Business" as rich as *res*
In all its various nuances, riffs, and analogues)
Is that "minds long exercised in business"
Have lost the power to talk to themselves.
Hence at the end of the business day,
Those same minds don't know what to do.
By leaving their solitude fallow,
They have relinquished the privilege of being alone.
In Diocletian's case, although he was never
Sufficiently magnanimous to concede
Himself the pleasures of study,
Nevertheless he found some consolation in gardening.
As a matter of fact, after being asked
To return to the throne, he said
He'd rather grow cabbages with his own hands
Than pursue the virtues and the vices of the law.
Gibbon says that Diocletian reigned for 21 years,
And that if he should be remembered for anything
He should be remembered for "his

Resolution of abdicating the empire . . ."
A resolution, sorry to say, infrequently
Imitated either by queens or by kings.
Hence Diocletian's distinction:
"Unlike most, he knew when to quit, and he did."